Raw Food

Beginners Complete Guide To Converting To A Natural Raw Food Diet

Nutritious Superfoods Recipes To Detox Your Body And Feel Energized And Revitalized

Introduction

I want to thank you and congratulate you for downloading the book, *"Raw Food Diet: Beginners Complete Guide To Converting To A Natural Raw Food Diet - Nutritious Superfoods Recipes To Detox Your Body And Feel Energized And Revitalized."*

This book contains proven steps and strategies on how to ease into a natural raw food diet with ease and detox your body, feel revitalized and make a real change.

What comes to mind when you think of a raw food diet? Perhaps this conjures up thoughts of eating salads, smoothies or raw vegetables that might not ordinarily be your everyday kind of food which you could see yourself eating on a regular basis. Maybe you're pondering why anyone would go on a raw food diet especially if this is to be considered as a long term possibility when there are so many delicious cooked foods out there.

Well, if you have such questions, let me start by telling you about how many incredible benefits that come with switching to a raw food diet. Think about it; do you know that cooking has been proven to make various healthy foods lose their nutritional values? This is one of the main problems with eating cooked foods and could possibly be the reason why you may be somewhat malnourished despite eating all the healthy foods out there. As such, if you switch to a raw food diet, you are essentially increasing the amount of nutrients that you take from the same foods since there is no cooking to cause loss of nutrients. That's not all; eating raw food can help you to lose weight, live a healthier life, deepen intuition, improve digestion, improve your sleep, increase your energy levels and much much more as you are about to find out.

If you are looking to transition to a raw food diet plan, this book will make the transition process effortless. You will discover exactly what you need to make the transition a successful one, how to prepare different raw foods along with some delicious raw food recipes that you can prepare to make the process easy for you.

Thanks again for downloading this book, I hope you enjoy it!

Medical Disclaimer

You understand that any information as found within this book is for general educational and informational purposes only. You understand that such information is not intended nor otherwise implied to be medical advice.

You understand that such information is by no means complete or exhaustive, and that as a result, such information does not encompass all conditions, disorders, health-related issues, or respective treatments. You understand that you should always consult your physician or other healthcare provider to determine the appropriateness of this information for your own situation or should you have any questions regarding a medical condition or treatment plan.

This information has not been evaluated or approved by the FDA and is not necessarily based on scientific evidence from any source. These statements have not been evaluated by the Food and Drug Administration (FDA). The products referred to in the book are intended to support general well-being and are not intended to treat, diagnose, mitigate, prevent, or cure any condition or disease.

You agree not to use any information in our book, including, but not limited to product descriptions, customer testimonials, etc. for the diagnosis and treatment of any health issue or for the prescription of any medication or treatment.

You acknowledge that all customer testimonials as found on in our book are strictly the opinion of that person and any results such person may have achieved are solely individual in nature; your results may vary.

You understand that such information is based upon personal experience and is not a substitute for obtaining professional medical advice. You should always consult your physician or other healthcare provider before changing your diet or starting an exercise program.

In light of the foregoing, you understand and agree that we are not liable nor do we assume any liability for any information contained within our book as well as your reliance on it. In no event shall we be liable for direct, indirect, consequential, special, exemplary, or other damages related to your use of the information contained within our book.

David Wilson's Publications

Below you'll find some of my other popular books that are popular on Amazon and Kindle as well. Simply go to the links to see more. Alternatively, you can visit my author page on Amazon to see other work done by me.

Vegan Cookbook: Vegan Diet With 50+ Vegan Recipes In The No1 Vegan Cookbook For Any Vegan Under Pressure. Delicious Vegan Recipes For Vegan Weight Loss, Vegan Bodybuilding And A Vegan Diet

Go to: http://amzn.to/1tosR4k

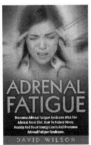

Adrenal Fatigue: Overcome Adrenal Fatigue Syndrome With The Adrenal Reset Diet. How To Reduce Stress, Anxiety And Boost Energy Levels And Overcome Adrenal Fatigue Syndrome

Go to: http://amzn.to/1U1a1GH

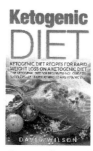

Ketogenic Diet: Ketogenic Diet Recipes For Rapid Weight Loss On A Ketogenic Diet. The Ketogenic Diet For Beginners No1 Guide To Successfully Transitioning To A Ketogenic Diet

Go to: http://amzn.to/1OowbWv

If the links do not work, for whatever reason, you can simply search for these titles on the Amazon website to find them.

Table of Contents

Raw Food Diet Demystified

A raw food diet mainly focuses on eating whole, fresh, unrefined, plant-based foods like vegetables, fruits, nuts, and seeds that are eaten in their natural state without steaming or cooking. You can also eat raw animal products and by products. The science behind this is that when you cook food you are actually killing the vital enzymes and destroying the nutritional value that make the food healthy and that is why this diet is also referred to as living diet. According to this diet food is seen to be raw if it is prepared or cooked below 116 degrees F because above this temperature range food starts to lose vital enzymes and nutrients.

The common misconception is that all raw food dieters are vegans; this is not true. It is important to point out that there are different types of raw food dieters. While most people on a raw food diet are vegetarians and vegans, some still eat raw meat.

So, how do you stand to benefit from going on a raw food diet. Let us look at this in the following section so that you can get the motivation to get started.

Benefits Of A Raw Food Diet
Weight loss

Protease and lipase are enzymes, which are abundantly found in raw foods and they aid in weight management. This is because lipase often assists your body in distributing, digesting and burning of fat while protease helps in breaking down proteins and getting rid of toxins. Without the help of lipase, fat often accumulates and stagnates. In addition, your body will not get rid of toxins effectively, which leads to the expansion of fat cells as toxins which are stored in fat cells and this leads to weight gain.

Improved immunity

In order for you to feel energized and handle whatever the day may bring, you abundantly depend on your immune system to keep you going and remaining strong and healthy. When you have a strong immunity then your body can fight off viruses, stay alert and awake, heal wounds, and attack anything that wants to harm your body. The healthier you are, the stronger your immune system and for this to happen you have to ensure that you pay attention and control what you consume. I know this is pointing out the obvious but you have the opportunity to transform your life with this knowledge.

Raw foods are also incredibly valuable because of their ability to help improve immune function due to the high concentration of antioxidants. These are substances that aid in preventing the damaging effects of oxidation on cells in your body. As stated in a research conducted by Penn State University, antioxidants such as polyphenols, vitamin C, E, A and minerals for example selenium boost your immunity by quenching highly-reactive compounds and free radicals which come from the environment or are formed as byproducts of normal processes in your body. By neutralizing these harmful radicals and compounds, antioxidants assist in reducing the risks of getting diseases such as diabetes, cancer, heart disease, and high blood pressure.

More energy

Eating raw foods will provide you with an unbelievable energy boost. This is because when you cook food above 116 degrees you kill enzymes that will help in boosting your energy. In addition, as you reduce your intake of highly processed foods and eat more raw foods, you will feel more energetic because of the high nutrient and enzyme content in raw foods. You will not even need stimulants like coffee.

In addition, digesting cooked food needs more energy than digesting raw food and this is because raw food is more easily digestible than cooked food; thus, it goes through the digestive tract in 1/3 or ½ of the same time which it would take cooked food. This in the end will provide you with much more energy, which you can enjoy and benefit from in your day-to-day life. Think about it. Imagine having an abundance of energy every single day from the moment you wake up to the moment you fall asleep.

Better digestion

Raw foods are high in fiber, which helps in improving the digestion and excretion of waste products in your body. Moreover, the body needs about twenty-two different enzymes, which help in digesting fats, proteins and carbohydrates; raw fruits and vegetables are a rich source for theses enzymes.

Some of these enzymes include amylase, which breaks down carbohydrates into sugar, lactase, which breaks down lactose in milk products, lipase, which breaks down fats into glycerol and fatty acids and protease, which breaks down proteins into amino acids.

On the contrary when you eat enzyme dead foods then you are putting a huge burden on your organs and pancreas and overworking them, which in the end can lead to health problems.

Combats anemia

Raw foods such as beets also help in fighting anemia but beets loose more than twenty-five percent of their folate when they are cooked. Folate is a water-soluble vitamin B, which assists in generating growth and production of new healthy cells, and when mixed with vitamin B 12 it aids your body in producing normal red blood cells. The lack of folate can lead to a decrease in your appetite and also can affect the tone of your skin. In the long run lack of folate can also lead to anemia, which is caused by your body having very few red blood cells and this will lead to less oxygen circulating in your body.

These are a selection of the most pertinent benefits. However there are so many more which relate to the environment, the earth, the welfare of animals, the psychological changes you will experience on a raw food diet, the prevention of disease and many many more. However like any diet or any major change you are likely to face challenges as you get started on the raw food diet and I want to make sure you feel prepared for these obstacles. Therefore, we are going to look at these challenges in the next chapter and see how you can deal with them in order to be successful in your raw food diet lifestyle.

Challenges And Concerns About The Raw Food Diet And How To Deal With Them

Consuming raw foods can be quite challenging especially for a first timer. Below are some of the challenges that are from time to time encountered and how to deal with them.

Freshness and availability of food

Depending on where you live getting your hands on produce, which you are after may sometimes be restricted by season. This could also be a problem if the foods are being shipped in from other far locations. However you can deal with these challenges by eating foods that are locally grown and in-season and a degree of flexibility is required here.

Additionally fresh, nutritious and delicious raw foods can sometimes become stale quicker than processed or dried foods and so therefore it is worthwhile ensuring you always have a supply of fresh raw foods on you. You may have find that you have to go shopping a little more frequently than usual. However this is a habit, which can quickly be changed as soon as you start believing and benefiting in the raw food diet.

Temptation

Going raw will require you to have will power, commitment, and determination, as there are not as many raw food dieters; hence, the temptation is real. To deal with this, ensure that you always stock up on delicious and fresh raw foods. Try as much as possible not to run out of food so the difficult moments when you could slip back into old eating habits are avoided. You should also have on you some raw food snacks that you can eat which require little or no preparation like bananas, carrots, apples, tomatoes, cucumbers, avocadoes, olives, and various kinds of seeds and nuts, which are high in healthy fats and will help you feel full; thus avoiding instances of gorging on cooked foods.

To retain the enthusiasm, improve your intake of nutrients and make sure that you give your taste buds some exciting new tastes. This means that it is important that you try and learn some new raw foods diet recipes.

Staying focused and being aware of the reasons why you are following this diet is a good way to remain committed. Many raw food dieters will say that the new sense of vibrancy and feelings of good health as well as being far more energetic throughout the day makes it worthwhile to adopt this diet.

Nutrition issues because of following a raw food diet

To enable your body to get the necessary nutrients, try to eat a large variety of fresh raw foods including different colored foods. You can also consume fresh raw foods that are in season as that would ensure that you get various kinds of raw foods all through the year.

To avoid getting nutritional deficiencies because of eating raw foods ensure that you chew food well as this will enable you to mix the food with the digestive enzymes and will increase surface area of the food as well as breaking down the vital compounds in the food. This will in the end lead to better digestion and absorption of nutrients.

Eating fully raw and plant based foods can also lead your body to lack adequate proteins (especially when vegan) however you can deal with this by consuming enough legumes, nuts, and seeds that are relatively high in protein. You should also ensure that you listen to your body.

Moreover, raw foods may be low in caloric content and you may therefore have to consume a variety of raw foods to meet your daily caloric needs. If you get yourself wanting to eat sweet food then you should eat more fruits or fresh fruit juice. As far as how much raw food you should consume, there is no need to restrict or limit yourself. This is because these foods have very high in fiber, water and nutrient content and it is quite impossible to overeat and become overweight on these foods.

Going raw while travelling

Consuming raw foods while travelling is very challenging. Therefore, to be on the safe side you have to plan ahead and look for restaurants and food stores that offer raw food produce in advance.

You can also carry foods such as bananas, raw nuts, apples, or even dried fruit to snack on just in case you are unable to find raw foods.

Getting used to raw foods

When shifting from a diet that mostly contains cooked foods to a raw food one, do this at your own speed. You might need time to adapt and adjust and therefore you should not rush yourself into making this transition quickly.

You should also know that when you first start taking raw foods you may begin experiencing some signs commonly referred to as detoxification reactions. These may include nausea, headaches, and tiredness; however, you should not get worried when this happens, as the symptoms will fade away slowly, when you body has cleaned itself out.

Generally, what you should know is that the more raw foods you consume and the longer you do this, the easier it becomes for you. Your taste buds and body will adjust slowly and you will love the energetic and light feeling that raw foods give you.

Since easing into the diet is one of the most common challenges faced by many dieters, we will address this comprehensively in the following chapter.

How To Ease Into The Diet

The best way to get used to raw foods is to slowly incorporate more raw vegetables and fruits into your diet. A good way to do this is to try to consume 75% raw foods and 25% lightly cooked foods. For instance, you can incorporate one or two raw meals into your diet like a salad and then build it up from there. Other tips to help you ease into the diet include:

Get informed about the raw foods diet

Learning more and more about the purpose and philosophy behind raw foods is a vital part in ensuring you stick to the diet and that you are benefiting as well as enjoying the diet.

In addition at the end of the day it is your health and body and therefore you have to be the informed consumer. This is because when going through the diet you will obviously encounter friends or members of your family who think that what you are doing is not worthwhile. It is completely okay for this to happen as most people get frightened by something they know very little about. Therefore its great if you have some in depth knowledge at your finger tips such as in this book so they can understand. This will ensure that when you come under attack and you are questioned about the diet, you are prepared and you have your answers prepared and ready.

Eliminate processed and refined foods from your diet

Get rid of refined and processed foods first before even thinking about following a raw foods diet. This will perhaps be the most beneficial thing that you would have done to your health and overall well being.

It is usually quite hard for someone to be addicted to cooked food but it is very easy for a person to be addicted to processed foods. Therefore, your first step to adopting a raw food diet is first getting rid of highly processed foods from your diet. Do this for approximately one month as you continue eating cooked meals. After a month, you can start substituting your meals with raw foods.

Planning is very important

Planning is actually very important for you to come out successful when following the diet. This is because you now have to prepare raw food recipes that you might not have ever done before and this can be very challenging for you. You also have to come up with various menus that will keep you going for the whole week. You can do this by searching various websites or reading raw food diet books that will give you brilliant ideas on the shopping lists that you will need to make the most delicious raw recipes.

The good thing though is that most raw food recipes are easy to prepare; thus, you don't have to worry about spending a lot of time preparing food.

Find a community

Lastly it is incredibly worthwhile when beginning this journey, to have a community, which helps in giving you support through ideas for recipes for example and generally acting act as your support system. There are various online forums that you can join and interact with fellow raw food dieters and have questions answered that you might not know about. There are also some raw foods dieters that you can connect with on Facebook or Twitter whom you can exchange messages or ideas that can spark interesting and insightful conversations and allow for an expansion of your circle of raw food friends. You can also look online for get togethers, cafes, raw food festivals and raw food classes. All this will help you stay strong while transitioning to a raw food diet.

Raw Breakfast Recipes

1. Vanilla Yogurt
Servings: 1

Ingredients

½ teaspoon of vanilla extract

1 cup of coconut meat

½ cup of coconut water

Steps

1. Open coconut using a cleaver then add the coconut water into a blender together with the coconut milk. Add in the extract and blend until you get a yoghurt consistency.

2. Serve and enjoy

2. Oat Meal
Servings: 2

Ingredients

Pure water

2 teaspoons of cinnamon

1 tablespoon of golden flax seed

1 banana

2 apples

Steps

1. Place flax seeds in the water and leave overnight.

2. Peel apples and slice them into small parts. Peel banana and chop into parts then rinse the flax seeds and place these ingredients into a blender. Add in ¼ cup of water to make it easier to blend then blend until the mixture is smooth.

3. You can add more water if the mixture is very thick.

3. Blueberry Smoothie
Servings: 2

Ingredients

½ teaspoon of green powder (optional)

Pure water

Liquid stevia (optional)

1 bag of frozen berries

1 tablespoon of flax seed

2 bananas

Steps

1. Place the ingredients in a blender then add in some pure water ensuring that the ingredients are entirely covered.

2. Pulse well; you can add more water if the mixture is very thick. You can blend the mixture longer if you find it very cold.

4. Carrot Juice
Servings: 1

Ingredients

½ lemon

2 pounds of carrots

1 bunch kale, washed

Steps

1. Wash lemon and slice most of the peel off then juice the lemon, kale and the carrots. Serve and enjoy.

5. Banana Pancakes
Servings: 1

Ingredients

2 tablespoons of dried coconut flakes

1 banana

Pinch of cinnamon

Steps

1. Smash the banana using a fork in a bowl until smooth then put in the cinnamon and coconut meal and combine well.

2. Flatten the coconut and banana dough and form small pancakes then leave then to dry in direct sunlight for around an hour. Flip the other side and leave for another hour, you can also use a dehydrator although this will take longer.

6. Avocado Apple Mousse

Servings: 2

Ingredients

¼ cup purified water

2 apples

1 avocado

Steps

1. Peel apples and get rid of the core then slice the avocado, remove the pit and scoop out the meat using a spoon.

2. Place these two ingredients in a bowl and combine well using a hand mixer. You can add in water to make the mouse slightly thinner.

7. Pear Muesli with Creamy Cashew Milk

Yields: 4½ cups cashew milk; 2 servings of muesli

Ingredients

For the creamy cashew milk:

Pinch of salt

1 teaspoon of vanilla extract

4 pitted medjool dates

3 cups of water

1 cup of raw cashews, soaked for at least 4 hours rinsed, and drained

For the ginger pear muesli:

Extra pear slices, for serving

1 small pear, grated

½ tablespoon of finely grated, fresh ginger

½ teaspoon of ground cinnamon

3 tablespoons of raisins (or another dried fruit of choice)

2 teaspoons of chia seeds

1 cup of rolled oats

Steps

For the cashew milk

Blend all of the ingredients in a high speed blender until smooth then put aside. You will have around 4 ½ cups of cashew milk.

For the muesli

Combine all of the ingredients for the muesli in a bowl then put in 1 ¾ cup of the cashew milk, stir to combine well.

Cover the mixture and leave it overnight in your fridge then the next day pour the muesli into bowls and add in the remaining cashew milk. Top with extra slices of pear and serve.

8. Fruit Combo

Servings: 1

Ingredients

1 peeled grapefruit with the segments cut from the membrane

1 peeled, halved and sliced kiwi

Fresh mint

2 oranges, 1 peeled and sliced and the other one segments cut from the membrane

Chopped cashews, optional

Steps

1. Combine the fruits and arrange them on a plate.

9. Pumpkin Chia Pudding with Vanilla Cream

Servings: 1

Ingredients

Chia layer

3 handfuls chia seeds

3 drops vanilla extract

1 pinch cayenne pepper

1 teaspoon extra virgin olive oil

5×1 cm fresh ginger root, peeled and grated

1 orange, juiced

2 tablespoons raw coconut cream (blend coconut meat with a little coconut water to form cream)

5 tablespoons raw pumpkin juice

Matcha Cream layer

½ teaspoon matcha green tea powder

15 drops organic vanilla extract

2 tablespoons brown rice syrup

3 tablespoons coconut cream

Steps

1. To make the chia layer, put, coconut cream, pumpkin puree, vanilla, cayenne, ginger, and orange juice in a food processor and puree until smooth. As you blend, add olive oil slowly.

2. Pour this liquid into a bowl, add the chia seeds then combine with a spoon ensuring that the chia seeds are covered with the liquid. Let this stir for an hour or overnight.

3. To make the matcha cream, place the vanilla, matcha, sweetener and coconut cream in a bowl and whisk until smooth.

4. Pour this over the chia layer and refrigerate for 30 minutes. If you don't have much time on your hands, simply sprinkle with fresh mint and enjoy.

10. Breakfast Balls
Makes: 16 balls

Ingredients

½ cup Medjool dates, chopped

¼ cup cranberries, chopped

¼ cup raisins, chopped

¼ cup date paste (blend 4 dates with 4 tablespoons water)

¼ cup yacon syrup

½ cup almonds, chopped

2 tablespoons melted coconut oil

½ cup desiccated coconut

½ cup shredded coconut

½ teaspoons cinnamon

1 cup raw almonds flour

Zest of orange

Juice of ½ orange

2 tablespoons hemp seeds

2 tablespoons chia seeds

Pinch of Himalayan sea salt

Steps

1. Whisk the orange juice with the zest and chia. Mix the other ingredients (except desiccated coconut) in a bowl.

2. Add the orange and chi mix and mix again. Work on the mixture using your hands until you get a nice consistency.

3. Roll into balls then roll into the desiccated coconut and put in the freezer to set before eating.

4. You can also dehydrate at 105∘F for around 8 hours for a crispier finish.

Raw Lunch Recipes

11. Carrot & Ginger Soup
Servings: 4

Ingredients

¼ teaspoon of salt

1 tablespoons white miso paste

1 cup of coconut water

1 cup of coconut meat

Pinch of cayenne pepper

1 tablespoon of chopped coriander

1 lemongrass stalk, sliced

1 tablespoon of sliced ginger

2 tablespoons of coconut nectar

Zest of one lime

¼ cup of lime juice

½ cup of cashew nuts soaked 20 minutes, drained

4 carrots

Sprigs of coriander to garnish

2 tablespoons of pumpkin seed oil to garnish (optional)

Steps

1. Mix all of the ingredients in a blender and pulse until smooth.

2. To make the mixture warm, blend in the blender for about 5 minutes. Season with some pepper and salt then garnish with some pumpkin seed oil and sprigs of coriander. Enjoy.

12. Mock Sushi

Servings: 8

Ingredients

1 tablespoon of lemon juice

Wasabi paste

2 tablespoons of tamari

Handful of coriander

1 cucumber

1 avocado

Snow pea sprouts

½ head of green cabbage

Raw Nori Sheets

Walnut Tuna

2 tablespoons of sesame seeds

1 carrot, chopped

2 tablespoons of chopped basil

2 tablespoons of chopped dill

½ chopped onion

3 tablespoons of minced parsley

1 cm piece of fresh ginger

1 teaspoon of garlic powder

3 tablespoons of tamari

3 tablespoons of extra virgin olive oil

3 tablespoons of lemon juice

3 cups of walnuts (soaked 4 hours then drained)

Steps

1. Put all of the ingredients apart from the sesame seeds, herbs and onion in a food processor and pulse until you form a paste. You can add some water if the mixture needs some binding.

2. Transfer the mixture to a bowl then stir in the sesame seeds, herbs and onion. Combine well and place in the refrigerator for about 5 days.

To assemble

3. Put a nori sheet the shiny side down on a chopping board then put a large piece of cabbage onto the nori sheet. Ensure that the edge of the cabbage is on the end of the nori   sheet close to you and covers the entire length of the nori sheet.

4. Top the cabbage with the tuna walnut mixture up to the ends and make it about one inch thick.

5. Add the sliced avocado, coriander, sliced cucumber, sprouts, dash of wasabi, lemon juice, and tamari. Spread the veggies along the length of the nori sheet then begin to carefully roll the sushi away from you ensuring that you keep pressure so that the contents remaining intact in the sushi.

6. When you have finished rolling, leave around one inch of the nori sheet at the end and put a dab of water to moisten the sheet. Roll to completely seal the sushi and cut it using a sharp knife into medium sized pieces. Serve.

13. Kale Citrus Salad and Tahini Dressing

Servings: 2

Ingredients

For the dressing

Salt + pepper to taste

2 teaspoons of orange zest

1 tablespoon of olive oil

1 tablespoon + 1 teaspoon of maple syrup

2 tablespoons of apple cider vinegar

2 tablespoons + 1 teaspoon of tahini

2-3 tablespoons of freshly squeezed orange juice

For the salad

Toasted + salted pumpkin seeds

1 apple, chopped

1 ruby red grapefruit, peeled + sliced

1 head lacinato kale

Steps

1. Put all of the ingredients for the dressing in a mixing bowl beginning with two tablespoons of

orange juice and stir vigorously until fully mixed. Add a pinch of pepper and salt then taste to know if more seasoning is required. The dressing will become thicker as it sits; therefore, you can add some more orange juice.

2. Remove the stems from the kale and wash, pat dry and chop them. Put the chopped kale in a bowl, add the dressing, and massage it into the greens using your hands.

3. Add more of the dressing as you want then put in pumpkin seeds, apple and grapefruit. Serve right away.

14. Noodles and Thai Peanut Sauce
Servings: 2-4

Ingredients

Rainbow Noodle Bowl

Mixed veggies of choice

2 tablespoons of peanuts

1 teaspoon of sesame seeds

2 zucchinis, spiralized

1 package 16 oz. of kelp noodles

Thai Peanut Sauce

½ teaspoon of red chili flakes

1 teaspoon of ginger

1 teaspoon of minced garlic

1 tablespoon of coconut vinegar

1 tablespoon of coconut aminos

2 tablespoons of date paste

3 tablespoons of raw peanut butter

1 lime, juice

¼ cup of water

Steps

1. Add all of the sauce ingredients in a bowl and mix together.

2. Rinse the noodles and combine with the spiralized zucchini in a mixing bowl. You can add in any of your favorite veggies for example green onions, edamame, purple cabbage, and bell peppers.

3. Add the sauce over the noodles and combine well then leave the sauce for about 10 minutes to marinate the veggies while mixing occasionally. Once you are ready to serve and eat, drizzle on top some peanuts and sesame seeds.

15. Veggie Nori Rolls
Servings: 1

Ingredients

Salt, to taste

1 teaspoon of lemon juice

1 tablespoon of nutritional yeast flakes

¼ avocado, sliced thinly

1 small Persian cucumber, cut into matchsticks

¼ cup of shredded carrots

¼ cup of sweet pea shoots or sprouts

2 tablespoons of hummus, tahini, or cashew cheese

1 sheet nori

Steps

1. Start by arranging the nori sheet on a working surface ensuring that the long edge is close to you. Then spread the hummus in a thin layer on top of the nori sheet.

2. Then proceed to layer the avocado, cucumber sticks, carrots and pea shoots right on top of the bottom third of the nori sheet and then sprinkle with some lemon juice and season this with salt to taste.

3. Next, proceed to gently but formly roll the edge that is closest to you towards the very center of the nori wrap ensuring to form a sushi like roll. You can use a sushi mat to make this a lot easier for you especially given that trying to do it freehand does require some practice.

4. Once done, use a sharp knife to slice the roll and serve immediately.

16. Living Raw Pizza
Servings: 4-6

Ingredients

Crust

½ cup of water or as needed

3-4 tablespoons of honey

1 1/2 teaspoons of salt

2 cloves of fresh garlic (chopped)

2 teaspoons of dried basil

2 tablespoons of olive oil

2 cups of sunflower seeds (ground fine)

2 cups of almonds (ground fine)

3/4 cup of golden flax seeds (ground fine)

Tomato Sauce

Salt to taste

1 tablespoons of lemon juice

3 dates (pitted)

2 tablespoons of olive oil

2 cloves of garlic (chopped)

1/2 teaspoon of thyme

1 teaspoon of dried oregano

3 teaspoons of dried basil

1 cup of sun dried tomatoes (soaked for 2 hrs, save soaked water)

8 roma tomatoes (chopped)

Ricotta cheese

2 cloves garlic

1 teaspoon of Celtic sea salt

1 tablespoon of lemon juice

1 cup pure water

1/2 cup truly raw cashews

1 cup almonds (soaked for 8 hrs.)

Steps

How to crust

1. Start by putting the olive oil, basil, salt, honey and water in a food processor then pulse everything until smooth and set aside.

2. Next, combine the sunflower seed powder, flax seed powder, and almond powder in a large mixing

bowl then proceed to pour the water mixture on top using your hands such that you form a big mound.

3. Next, add in some more water if you have to then knead the dough to help you form a smooth round. You can then taste the mixture for seasonings and adjust the salt if necessary.

4. Next, proceed to divide the mound into four sections then form these into balls. For the first ball, put it onto a teflex sheet, then shape it into a thin round that is about 4mm thick. For the 'lip' (crust) that's around the pizza, ensure to make it a little thicker then do the same thing for each of the other mounds. Then place each of the pizza into a dehydrator then set the temperature to 105 degrees F for about 10 hours. Once done, remove from teflex sheet then continue to dehydrate on the tray for another 10 hours. Ensure to leave the pizzas inside the dehydrator until you are ready to put the sauce and the toppings on.

How to sauce

5. Simply place everything inside a blender, ad in the tomato soak water and then blend until it is thick and then set aside.

How to cheese

6. Simply blend everything together until you have a smooth and thick consistency. Then add in some salt if necessary and then place the mixture in a glass bowl, and cover it with a clean cloth. Allow it to stand for about 6 hours at room temperature.

Assembly

7. If you can, try serving the pizzas in pizza boxes. To do that, simply take one pizza, place it in a box, spread the tomato sauce on the pizza crust that you formed, add in some dollops of cheese all around and then throw some toppings on top. Proceed to garnish with edible flowers and then close the lid of the box. You can then decorate the box if you want to then enjoy while warm with a light salad.

17. Spaghetti and Meatballs
Servings: 2-3

Ingredients

Spaghetti

2-4 green and yellow zucchini sliced on a saladacco, tossed in a little lemon juice and set aside.

Sauce

1 teaspoon of sea salt

1 teaspoon of Italian seasoning

1 handful of fresh basil

1 pinch of fresh oregano

3 tablespoon of fresh parsley

2 cloves of garlic

3 tablespoons of olive oil

2 dates (soaked for 2 hrs)

1 teaspoon of tomato concentrate

1 cup of sun dried tomatoes (soaked for 1-2 hrs)

2 cups of cherry tomatoes

Savory Nut Balls

2 teaspoons of dried cilantro

1 teaspoon of cumin

Pinch of turmeric

1 stick of celery (minced)

2 cloves of garlic

¼ cup of walnuts

½ cup of soaked sunflower seeds

1 cup of soaked almonds

1 cup of burdock puree (you can blend it with the water or grate it on a very fine grater)

2 carrots

1 bell pepper

1 small red onion

Steps

Sauce

1. How to: Simply blend everything together until it is smooth then add in the tomato soak water if you want to make the sauce a bit thinner. Next, proceed to toss with the 'spaghetti' then serve along with savory nut balls.

Savory Nut Balls

2. Simply process everything together inside a food processor and add some little water if necessary. Place a parchment paper on the table then put the burger mixture on top of this. Proceed to get another piece of parchment paper and then put it on top of the mixture. Using the palms of your hand or a rolling pin, ensure to roll the dough to ½ inch thickness.

3. Then use a cup or a cookie cutter to cut out patty shapes then place these patties on teflex sheets. Next, dehydrate inside an exchalibur dehydrator for about 2 hours at about 145 degrees F (only inside the exhalibur at this temperature).

4. Next, bring the temperature down to about 115 degrees F then continue dehydrating until you arrive at the desired consistency.

18. Raw Stuffed Mushrooms with Rosemary Garlic "Cream"

Servings: 4

Ingredients

Stuffed Mushrooms

Himalayan salt and pepper to taste

½ cup of pine nuts

½ cup of kalamata olives, chopped

4 cups of spinach, crushed

2 tablespoons of coconut nectar

¼ cup plus 2 tablespoons of tamari

1 cup of diced sweet onion, divided

3 cups of diced tomato, divided

4 large portobello mushroom caps

Cashew Garlic Cream

Himalayan salt and pepper to taste

1 teaspoon of fresh rosemary, finely chopped

1 clove of garlic

1/2 cup of water

1 cup of cashews, soaked overnight, drained and rinsed

Steps

For the mushrooms

Start by rubbing 2 tablespoons of tamari on the mushroom caps inside as well as outside. Then place half the onions and the tomatoes in a bowl. Once done, stir in the coconut nectar and the remaining ¼ cup of tamari- ensure all the onions and tomatoes are nicely coated. Next, proceed to spread everything on a non-stick dehydrator sheet then dehydrate at 115 degrees for about 2-4 hours.

Then when the onions and tomatoes are nicely done, proceed to mix them together with the remaining pine nuts, olives, spinach, onions, and the remaining tomatoes. Then season with pepper and salt to taste. Proceed to spoon the tomato mixture into the mushroom caps then top this with the garlic cashew cream.

For the garlic cream

Simply blend the garlic, water, and cashews inside a high speed blender until it is smooth then stir in the pepper, salt and rosemary.

19. Stuffed Kale Leaves with Cashew Aioli

Servings: 2

Ingredients

For the stuffing

½ cup of organic raisins (diced)

2 cups organic fresh mint (minced and tightly packed)

1 cup of organic sun-dried tomatoes (diced)

5 sprigs of organic green onions

1 teaspoon of Himalayan pink salt

2 tablespoons of organic lemon juice (fresh squeezed)

½ teaspoon of organic ground cinnamon

3 teaspoons of organic lemon zest

½ cup of organic pine nuts

1 clove of organic garlic

½ cup of organic extra-virgin olive oil

3 cups of raw organic cauliflower

For the aioli

1/3 cup of organic mint leaves (tightly packed)

½ cup of purified or distilled water

5 cloves of organic garlic

1 teaspoon of organic lemon zest

½ teaspoon of organic maple syrup (or organic raw honey)

½ teaspoon of Himalayan pink salt

1 ¼ tablespoon of organic lemon juice (fresh squeezed)

1 cup of organic raw cashews

Steps

1. Prepare the stuffing: Pulse the cauliflower in a food processor until it achieves a rice-like consistency. Transfer to a bowl and set aside.

2. Add all the ingredients for the stuffing (except the mint leaves, sun-dried tomatoes, and raisins) into a blender and blend until creamy.

3. Add this mixture to the cauliflower and mix using your hand.

4. Add the mint leaves, raisins and sun-dried tomatoes, to the mixture and mix again by hand.

5. To prepare the aioli: Put all ingredients (except the mint) into a blender and blend until creamy.

6. Transfer to a small bowl and stir in the mint leaves by hand to ensure they remain visible in the aioli.

7. To prepare the kale leaves and assemble: Cut off the bottom stem part of the kale and using a spatula, spread a tablespoon or two of the stuffing onto the leaf and roll up.

8. Serve with the aioli and enjoy!

20. Save-the Turkey Portobello Mushroom
Servings 4-6

Ingredients

Dash or two of water

A few grinds of fresh black pepper

2 teaspoons of poultry seasonings

2 tablespoons of gluten free tamari, Namya Shoyu or Braggs Aminos

4 tablespoons of Olive oil

3-4 large Portobello mushroom caps

Steps

Start by carefully removing the stems from the Portobello mushrooms then use a damp paper towel to wipe the mushrooms. Then proceed to slice each mushroom into ½ inch strips.

Then inside a small bowl, whisk the black pepper, water, poultry seasoning, tamari and olive oil then place the mushroom strips in a baking dish then pour the marinade over each mushroom. Then proceed to marinate for about 20-30 minutes ensuring to turn occasionally. Keep in mind that mushrooms are spongy so you may have to add some more marinade after some time.

Then place a baking dish inside a dehydrator until it is warm i.e. for about 1- 1.5 hours. It is best served warm but delicious in whichever way you serve it. If you don't have any dehydrator, you can place it inside an oven on the lowest possible temperature while the door is slightly open. Try testing in 15 minutes to see if the mushrooms feel somewhat warm to touch.

Raw Dinner Recipes

21. Red Cabbage and Apple Salad with Ginger Vinaigrette
Servings: 4

Ingredients

¼ cup of toasted, unsalted sunflower seeds

¼ cup of golden raisins, plumped in hot water

2 teaspoons of fresh lemon juice

2 cups of thinly sliced Granny Smith apple

2 cups of packed shredded Napa cabbage

2 cups of packed shredded red cabbage

1/8 teaspoon of ground black pepper

¼ teaspoon of kosher salt

3 tablespoons of extra-virgin olive oil

½ teaspoon of minced garlic

1 teaspoon of honey

1 teaspoon of Dijon mustard

1 1/2 teaspoons of grated peeled fresh ginger

3 tablespoons of apple cider vinegar

Steps

1. Start by whisking together the last five ingredients (starting from garlic) in pepper, salt and olive oil then set this aside. Then toss the cabbages together inside a large serving bowl. Proceed to toss the apple slices with lemon juice to ensure they don't start browning.

2. Next, half of the sunflower seeds, raisins and the apple to the cabbage then toss it with dressing and finally garnish with the remaining seeds.

22. Thai Coleslaw
Servings: 4

Ingredients

2 tablespoons of honey

Himalaya sea salt

1 handful of torn basil leafs

1 handful of cilantro leafs

1 ripe mango, cut in small dices

¼ cup of carrots, shredded

¼ cup of red cabbage, shredded

½ head white cabbage, shredded

1 cup of raw almond or peanut butter

1 ½ tablespoon of tamari

½ tablespoon of red chili

2 tablespoons of chopped ginger

½ cup of lemon juice

½ cup of raw cashews

Steps

1. Start by cutting the mango into small cubes then shed the carrots and the cabbage. Next, puree the braggs aminos, red chili, ginger, lemon juice, and honey in a high speed blender (e.g. vita mix). Then add the raw almond butter and then proceed to blend at low speed to combine or until you have a cake batter like consistency. If you want to make it thinner, you can add in some water.

2. Proceed to mix the raw almond butter mixture and the cabbage really well then add the mango pieces and the raw cashews. Finally, you can top with basil or cilantro leaves along with a few pieces of carrots and or mango for color.

23. Jalapeño Gazpacho with Feta
Servings: 3

Ingredients

½ cup crumbled feta cheese, for garnish

Kosher salt

1 cup of tomato juice

Juice of 2 limes

¼ cup of red wine vinegar

¼ cup of chopped fresh mint leaves

¼ cup of flat-leaf parsley leaves, chopped

1 garlic clove, peeled and minced

½ jalapeño, minced

¾ cup of diced vidalia onion

2 seedless cucumbers, peeled and chopped

2 cups of cubed seedless watermelon

6 plum tomatoes, chopped

Steps

1. Blend all the ingredients (excluding the feta and the salt) in a blender or food processor until you have the desired consistency then season with salt.

2. Next, pour the mixture into serving bowls then garnish of them with 2 tablespoons of crumbled feta.

24. Mango Red Pepper Salsa
Servings: 1

Ingredients

Salt and pepper to taste

Dash of cayenne pepper

3 tablespoons of fresh lime juice

3 tablespoons of fresh cilantro leaves, chopped

3 tomatoes

½ red onion, chopped

1 red pepper, diced

2 ripe mangoes, peeled and diced

Steps

1. Simply combine all the ingredients in a bowl then cover nicely and let it to sit inside the fridge for about 1 hour (you could even refrigerate it overnight to make it taste better).

2. Serve it with raw crackers.

25. Carrot, Cabbage & Raisin Salad
Servings: 2

Ingredients

2 teaspoons of toasted sesame oil

Juice of 1 lemon

2 tablespoons of sesame seeds

¼ cup of raisins

3 grated carrots

½ head cabbage, sliced very thinly

Steps

1. Simply add all the ingredients to a bowl, then toss, let it marinade for some time to let the flavors meld together.

26. Green Peanut Soup
Servings: 1-2

Ingredients

Juice 1/8 lemon

A handful of basil

1 teaspoon of ginger, grated

1 garlic clove, chopped

A handful of leek, sliced

1 cup of spinach, fresh or frozen

1 cup of broccoli, fresh or frozen

2 cups of water

0.4 cups of raw peanuts

Salt to taste

Black and white pepper

Steps

1. Blend the peanuts to form a fine powder. Add water and blend again

2. Add the remaining ingredients and blend until you form a smooth consistency.

3. Garnish with whatever toppings you like, like nuts, seeds, or fresh herbs.

27. Tomato Basil Zucchini Pasta
Servings: 4

Ingredients

1 garlic clove, minced

¼ cup of walnuts, roughly chopped + extra for garnish

¼ medium onion, diced – yield ¼ cup

½ cup of nutritional yeast + extra for garnish

½ cup of packed fresh basil leaves, stems removed

2 fresh tomatoes – I used hot house

2 cups of sun dried tomatoes soaked in a cup of boiling water

4 zucchinis, nibby ends removed

Freshly ground black pepper, to taste

1 teaspoon of Himalayan rock salt, or to taste

1 teaspoon of dried oregano

Steps

1. Soak the tomatoes for 5 minutes in boiling water.

2. In the meantime, mix all the ingredients in a food processor except the walnuts.

3. Remove the tomatoes after five minutes and add them to the food processor with 1 cup of the soaking water.

4. Process for 2 minutes or until you achieve a smooth consistency. Remove from the food processor, then stir in walnuts.

5. To make your pasta, cut zucchini into half vertically then use a spiral slicer to make long strands. You can shred with a handheld grater if you don't have a spiral slicer.

6. Divide the zucchini among 4 plates then top with sauce and some extra walnuts.

28. Avocado and Corn Soup
Servings: 4

Ingredients

½ cup of green onion, chopped

4 ounces of lump crab meat, optional

½ cup of cherry tomatoes, chopped

Salt, to taste

Juice of 1 lime

1 jalapeño pepper, seeded, ribbed, and finely chopped

1 garlic clove

2 large avocados, pitted and diced

3 large sweet ears of corn, shucked

Steps

1. Hold the corn to a cutting board then carefully cut down and through the kernels.

2. Use your knife's spine to cut around an entire cob to remove any leftover corn pieces and liquid. Reserve ½ cup of corn kernels in a bowl and set aside.

3. Use a juicer to extract juice from the remaining kernels.

4. Combine garlic clove, half lime juice, half diced jalapeno and ½ cup corn juice in a blender and blend until smooth. Add the remaining corn juice and 2 avocados and blend until smooth.

5. Add more avocado if too thin and if it is too thick, add water.

6. Season with salt then refrigerate until when ready to serve.

7. To make the salsa combine tomatoes, remaining jalapeno, corn kernels, lime juice and salt to taste.

8. To assemble divide the soup among 12 glasses then top with heaping tablespoon salsa. Garnish with green onions.

29. Black Sesame Carrots with Avocado and Citrus Dressing
Servings: 6-8

Ingredients

For the salad

½ ripe avocado, peeled + chopped

Salt + pepper

Big handful of cilantro leaves, roughly chopped

¼ cup black sesame seeds

1 cup frozen shelled edamame, thawed

5-6 carrots, peeled + cut into matchsticks

For the ginger citrus dressing

¼ - 1/3 cup of grape seed oil

Couple drops of toasted sesame oil

1 inch piece of ginger, peeled and grated finely on a micro plane

1 ½ tablespoons of agave nectar

Salt + pepper

Juice of 1 lime

¼ cup of fresh orange juice

Steps

1. Mix the thawed edamame, cilantro, sesame seeds and carrot in a bowl and season with pepper and salt, then toss lightly with your hands and put aside.

2. Combine pepper, salt, sesame oil, ginger, agave nectar lime juice and orange juice in a small bowl and whisk until incorporated. As you whisk, drizzle the grapeseed oil slowly until you have a homogenous dressing.

3. Pour the dressing over the carrots and toss to mix. Top with avocado and garnish with cilantro and sesame seeds.

Raw Desserts

30. Raw Brownie
Servings: 8

Ingredients

¼ teaspoon of sea salt

2 tablespoons of honey or agave nectar

4 tablespoons of shredded unsweetened coconut

5 tablespoons of raw cacao (cocoa) powder

1 cup of dates

1 cup of pecans

Steps

1. Put the pecans in a food processor and pulse until they become crumbly and small then add in the dates and pulse again until the dates are processed well and the mixture sticks together.

2. Add in the remaining ingredients and pulse again until the mixture becomes dark chocolate brown. Ensure that you do not pulse too much to avoid it being too buttery.

3. Transfer the mixture to a cake pan and press it down with your hands then place in the refrigerator for some few hours.

4. Remove from the refrigerator, slice and enjoy. Store the brownies in the refrigerator for them to last longer.

31. Cherry Almond Balls
Yields: 18 balls

Ingredients

¼ cup of dried cherries, chopped

¼ cup of unsweetened coconut

1 cup of rolled oats

1 teaspoon of cinnamon

1 tablespoon of maple syrup

1 cup of cottage cheese

1 cup of raw almonds

Steps

1. Grind the almonds in a food processor until the mixture forms a coarse powder then add in cinnamon, maple syrup, and cottage cheese. Pulse until a paste like mixture forms.

2. In another bowl combine coconut, cherries and rolled oats then pour the wet ingredients into the dry ingredients and combine well.

3. Make the batter into 18 balls and put on a wooden chopping board with some parchment paper.

4. Put in the refrigerator and freeze for about 30 minutes. When ready to eat remove from the

refrigerator and leave it to thaw for around five minutes then enjoy.

32. Coconut Chia Pudding
Servings: 1

Ingredients

½ tablespoon of honey

1 cup of full-fat coconut milk

¼ cup of chia seeds

Steps

1. Combine honey, coconut milk, and chia seeds in a bowl and leave it to set in the refrigerator for about 24 hours.

2. Remove from the refrigerator and ensure that the pudding is thick and the chia seeds have gelled. Top with some nuts and fresh fruits, and eat right away.

33. Raw Strawberry Shortcake Pies
Servings: 10

Ingredients

Crust

2/3 cup of dates

1 cup of dried coconut

1 cup of cashews

Filling

4 cups of strawberries (reserve)

¼ cup of lemon juice

½ cup of honey

½ cup of coconut oil

2 cups of strawberries (to blend)

2 cups of cashews

Steps

To make the crust

1. Put the cashews and coconut in a food processor and pulse until the mixture is flour-like then add in the dates.

2. Process again for another 3 minutes until the mixture begins to get clingy and oily-ish. Stop processing when the mixture sticks together when pinched. Press the mixture into tart pan and put aside.

To make the filling

3. Put all of the filling ingredients in a high speed blender apart from the strawberries and cashews. Blend until the mixture is smooth then add in the cashews and blend again until the mixture is smooth.

4. Pour the filling mix into a bowl then chop finely the strawberries and gently stir using a spoon. Scoop the mix into tarts and enjoy.

34. Raw Cheesecake Hearts
Servings: 12

Ingredients

¾ cup of water

1/8 teaspoon of sea salt

2 tablespoons of lemon juice

1 teaspoon of pure vanilla extract

¼ cup of coconut oil

½ cup of maple syrup

½ cup of cocoa powder

2 ½ cups of cashews

Steps

1. Put all the ingredients in a high-speed blender and blend beginning with slow speed then slowly increase the speed. Blend until the mixture resembles creamy chocolate fudge and is smooth with no cashew chunks.

2. Pour the mix into final molds and put in the freezer then freeze until it sets for around 8 hours.

3. Store in the refrigerator and when you want to eat, slice, and eat right away.

35. Raw Drop Cookies
Servings: 8

Ingredients

½ teaspoon of Celtic sea salt

1 teaspoon of pure vanilla extract

½ cup of coconut oil (liquid)

½ cup of maple syrup

½ cup of tahini

2 cups of dried, shredded coconut

Steps

1. Put all the ingredients in a bowl apart from the shredded coconut and mix well using a spoon. When well mixed add in the shredded coconut and mix again using a spoon until well mixed.

2. Make balls using the dough and flatten them out to form cookies then place them on a cookie sheet.

3. Cover the cookies and freeze them for about 30 minutes until they become hard. Store the remaining cookies in the freezer.

36. Raw Raspberry Truffles
Yields: 12 truffles

Ingredients

Filling

½ cup of freeze-dried raspberries

¼ cup of filtered water

1 teaspoon of pure vanilla extract

1 teaspoon of pure almond extract

A pinch of sea salt

2 tablespoons of raw coconut nectar

½ cup of coconut butter, warmed to liquid

¼ cup of shredded coconut

2 cups of finely shredded coconut

Raw chocolate

A pinch of sea salt

¼ cup of raw coconut nectar

¾ cup of cacao powder

½ cup of cacao butter, warmed to liquid

Steps

1. Add the shredded coconut in a blender and pulse until it becomes fine flour, put aside.

2. Put coconut nectar, coconut butter, almond butter, water, extracts and sea salt in a food processor and process until the mixture is smooth.

3. Add into the food processor the pulsed coconut and process until a smooth dough is formed then freeze the mixture for around 30 minutes.

4. Mix all of the chocolate ingredients until the mixture is smooth then form balls using the dough and dip them into the chocolate mixture. Leave the excess chocolate to drain off and place on a foil then put in the freezer for around 5 minutes until the chocolate becomes hard.

37. Berry and Chia Sorbet
Servings: 4

Ingredients

A drizzle of agave syrup

3 tablespoons of chia seeds

2 cups of frozen berries

Steps

1. Put all the ingredients into a blender and blend until the mixture is smooth.

2. Serve right away, enjoy.

38. Walnut Cookies
Yields: 24 cookies

Ingredients

1 cup of chopped walnuts

1 tablespoon of vanilla

1/3 cup of agave

1/3 cup of water

1/3 cup of olive oil

½ cup of cacao powder

½ cup of ground flax

2 cups of almond flour

Steps

1. Combine cacao powder and almond flour then add in agave, oil, vanilla, and water. Stir to mix well then add in the chopped walnuts.

2. Form the mixture into balls using your palms then press them flat.

3. Put on a dehydrator and dehydrate for an hour at 145°F then reduce to 115 F and dehydrate for about 5-6 hours until you get the desired dryness.

39. Avocado and Coconut Popsicles
Servings: 4-6

Ingredients

1 teaspoon of vanilla extract

2 teaspoons of freshly squeezed lime juice

¼ cup of coconut nectar

¼ cup of coconut oil

400ml of organic coconut milk

2 ripe avocados

Steps

1. Mix all of the ingredients in a blender and pulse until the mixture is creamy.

2. Pour the mixture into popsicle molds and place in the refrigerator. Freeze for about 1 ½ - 2 hours. To remove the popsicles smoothly from the molds you can run the molds under warm water.

Raw Snacks

40. Raw Lemon Bars
Yields: 8 bars

Ingredients

¾ teaspoon of sea salt

1 ¼ cups of shredded dried coconut

2 tablespoons of lemon juice

2 tablespoons of lemon zest

1 tablespoon of pure vanilla extract

1 ½ cups of dates

1 cup of almonds

Steps

1. Put the almonds in a food processor and pulse into a fine powder then add in lemon juice, dates, lemon zest, and vanilla. Pulse until well combined then put aside.

2. Put salt and dried coconut in a bowl and combine using a spoon then pour this mixture into the food processor mix. Combine everything together using your hands to ensure everything is well mixed, the mixture will resemble a dough.

3. Transfer the dough into a glass dish and press the mix down into the glass dish using your hands to ensure that the mixture sticks together well.

4. Refrigerate the bar for around an hour so that they stick together well and are easy to cut. Garnish with some thawed or fresh strawberries. Store the bars in the refrigerator.

41. Vegan Chocolate Bars

Yields: 12 bars

Ingredients

¼ cup of dairy-free chocolate chips (optional)

1/3 cup of maple syrup

5 ounces of plant-based vanilla protein powder

1 ½ cups of rolled oats

1 teaspoon of cinnamon

¼ teaspoon of sea salt

1 cup of raw almonds

Steps

1. Line an eight by eight inch skillet with cooking spray and measure ¼ cup of almonds, slice them and put aside.

2. Put ¾ cup of the almonds and salt in a food processor and pulse for some minutes until you get almond butter.

3. Put in cinnamon, maple syrup, protein powder and oats, process until the mixture is smooth. Press mixture into the prepared skillet with a spoon and top using the sliced almonds.

4. Put chocolate chips in a glass bowl and microwave until the chocolate has melted then drizzle over the bars.

5. Place the bars in the fridge for them to set for about 20 minutes before slicing. Serve and enjoy and the remainder you should store in an airtight container in your fridge.

42. Pecan Pie Balls
Yields: 10-12 balls

Ingredients

½ teaspoon of pure vanilla extract

½ teaspoon of sea salt

1 cup of pecans

1 cup of packed and pitted dates

Steps

1. Put all the ingredients into a food processor and process until a dough is formed.

2. Remove the mixture from the processor and roll into small balls. Place in the fridge until when ready to serve them.

43. Fruit Skewers
Servings: 5

Ingredients

20 skewers

1 apple, cut into chunks

2 bananas, peeled and cut into chunks

¼ cantaloupe, cut into balls or cubes

5 large strawberries, halved

Steps

1. Thread the apple pieces, strawberries, banana, and cantaloupe alternately onto the skewers, putting around 2 pieces of each fruit on each skewer.

2. Place on a platter, enjoy.

44. Chocolate Nut Bites
Yields: 25 bites

Ingredients

Pinch of salt

2 tablespoons of cacao powder

2 tablespoons of coconut oil

1/3 cup of almond butter

1 cup (130g) of raw cashews

2 cups (300g) of dates

Steps

1. Put all the ingredients in a food processor and pulse for some minutes. The mixture will be at first crumbly but as you continue blending it will become a sticky dough that holds together when making a ball.

2. Roll the mixture into small balls using your palms and coat them with some cinnamon, coconut, crushed nuts or cocoa.

3. Put in the fridge and leave for around 1-2 hours for them to chill.

45. Radish Snack
Servings: 4

Ingredients

1 sprig of fresh cilantro, for garnish (optional)

¼ teaspoon of ground mixed peppercorns

1 teaspoon of salt

1 bunch of radishes, trimmed

Steps

1. Put the radishes in a medium mixing bowl and drizzle with peppercorns and salt.

2. Toss to mix well then garnish with fresh cilantro.

46. Kale Chips with Honey
Servings: 5

Ingredients

1 tablespoon of honey

½ lemon, juiced

1 teaspoon of sea salt

¼ cup of olive oil

2 bunches of dino kale, cut into 2-inch pieces

Steps

1. Mix the kale pieces with some sea salt, lemon juice, and olive oil in a resealable bag then seal.

2. Massage the mixture for around three minutes; the kale will slightly break down. Sprinkle some honey over the mixture and massage for three more minutes.

3. Place the kale flat on a food dehydrator and dehydrate for around 8 hours at 115 degrees F until they become crispy. Serve and enjoy.

47. Caramel Chocolate Apples
Servings: 4-6

Ingredients

4-6 apples

For the chocolate sauce

¼ cup of nut butter

½ cup of almond milk

¼ cup of dates

4 tablespoons of cacao

For the caramel

Seeds from ½ vanilla bean

1/8 teaspoon of salt

1/8 teaspoon of cinnamon

3 tablespoons of nut butter

1 cup of dates

½ cup of water

Steps

1. To make the sauce, blend all the ingredients for the chocolate sauce and pour into bowls.

2. To make the caramel, add all the caramel ingredients into a blender and pulse until smooth, and scoop into bowls.

3. Dip the apples into the chocolate sauce then the caramel sauce and enjoy.

48. Cucumbers with Fresh Dill
Servings: 6-8

Ingredients

½ teaspoon of freshly ground black pepper

3 tablespoons of sugar

¼ cup of finely chopped fresh dill

½ cup of distilled white vinegar

1 tablespoon of coarse kosher salt

2 English hothouse cucumbers, very thinly sliced and un-peeled

Steps

1. Put the cucumber slices in a colander and sprinkle some salt ensuring that you fully coat the slices.

2. In the meantime prepare the dressing; combine in a bowl sugar, pepper, vinegar and dill until all the sugar has been dissolved.

3. Drain the cucumbers well and pat them dry then put them into the bowl with the dressing and stir to coat them well. Place in the refrigerator for around 15 minutes- 2 hours then serve the cucumbers cold.

49. Raw Cheese Crackers with Peanut Butter

Ingredients

1 tablespoon of maple syrup

1 teaspoon of white miso

1 cup of water

¼ cup of coconut oil, melted

1 ½ cups of almonds, soaked for 8-10 hours, rinsed and drained

1 apple, cored and cut into chunks

2 medium-sized carrots, peeled and cut into chunks

½ cup of nutritional yeast

¼ cup of raw coconut flour

1 cup of flaxseed meal

Steps

1. Mix together coconut flour, nutritional yeast, and flax seed meal in a bowl and put aside.

2. Process the almonds in a food processor until crumbly in texture ensuring that you do not over do it, as you will get almond butter instead.

3. Add the almond meal into the bowl with the flax seed mix then put the apple and carrots in the processor and process until you get a nice mushy mixture. Add this mixture into the bowl with the flax seed and almond mixture.

4. Add into the bowl all the remaining ingredients and whisk until well mixed and the mixture holds together when pressed and should be slightly moist.

5. Separate the mixture into two then spread one of the halves on a dehydrator lined with nonstick drying sheet. To ensure that the dough has an even surface, cover the dough with another nonstick sheet then using a rolling pin; evenly and gently roll it out.

6. Remove carefully the nonstick sheet and when the dough is rolled out, score gently the surface into squares. Put the tray at the center of the dehydrator and set the temp to about 145 F then dehydrate for around 30 minutes.

7. Reduce the heat to around 115 F then dehydrate for another 6-8 hours until the crackers are extremely crispy. Repeat the same process for the remaining dough.

50. Berries & Jicama Salsa
Yields: 3 cups

Ingredients

2 tablespoons of finely chopped jalapeno pepper, stemmed and seeded

¼ cup of finely chopped red onion

1/3 cup of chopped cilantro

1 cup of diced jicama

1 cup of diced strawberries

1 cup of fresh blueberries

Salt, to taste

Juice of 1 large lime

Steps

1. Combine together strawberries, jicama, blue berries, lime juice, cilantro, jalapeno and red onion.

2. Stir until well mixed then season with some salt, serve, and enjoy.

Conclusion

Thank you again for downloading this book!

I hope this book was able to help you to learn more about the raw food diet and how to be successful while on the diet. The next step is to start replacing 1 or 2 of your daily cooked meals with raw meals in order to ease into the diet if you are a beginner. If you are not new to the raw food diet, this book has provided you with many recipes that you can try out. I wish you all the very best on your voyage with to becoming a healthier and happier you. The next step must be taken by you!

Thank You

Before you go, I'd like to say 'thank you' for purchasing my book. You could have picked from multiple books on the subject but you decided to give mine a chance.

So again, thanks for downloading my book and reading it all the way through. Now I would like to ask a small request of you which will take about 60 seconds of your time. Could you take a minute and kindly leave a review for this book on amazon.

Go to http://amzn.to/1OgfXyJ

This feedback will help me to continue to write kindle books that really make a difference. So if you enjoyed it, please let me know! Thank you and good luck!

Preview Of Vegan Cookbook - With 50+ Vegan Recipes In The No1 Vegan Cookbook For Any Vegan Under Pressure. Delicious Vegan Recipes For Vegan Weight Loss, Vegan Bodybuilding And A Vegan Diet

Description:

"Are you looking for more recipes to broaden your selection of delicious vegan meals? When you purchase "Vegan Cookbook" you'll find yourself equipped with a variety of **vegan recipes**, which make cooking vegan meals **easy**, **enjoyable** and **hassle free**. Inside you will find over 50+ **flavoursome**, **mouth watering** and **delicious** vegan recipes. Everything you need to **easily** prepare a ton of vegan food is right here. So eliminate endless decision-making and follow **easy** to prepare, **healthy** and **nourishing** vegan recipes. Enjoy all the incredible **benefits** of following a vegan diet and share your excitement for vegan food with others and enjoy these **fresh**, **new** and **delicious** vegan recipes."

Go to http://www.amzn.to/1tosR4k

David Wilson's Publications

Below you'll find some of my other popular books that are popular on Amazon and Kindle as well. Simply go to the links below to see more. Alternatively, you can visit my author page on Amazon to see other work done by me.

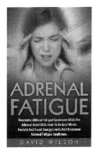 Adrenal Fatigue: Overcome Adrenal Fatigue Syndrome With The Adrenal Reset Diet. How To Reduce Stress, Anxiety And Boost Energy Levels And Overcome Adrenal Fatigue Syndrome

Go to: http://amzn.to/1U1a1GH

 Ketogenic Diet: Ketogenic Diet Recipes For Rapid Weight Loss On A Ketogenic Diet. The Ketogenic Diet For Beginners No1 Guide To Successfully Transitioning To A Ketogenic Diet

Go to: http://amzn.to/1OowbWv

If the links do not work, for whatever reason, you can simply search for these titles on the Amazon website to find them.

Printed in Great Britain
by Amazon